Mother's Thoughts for the Day

Mother's Thoughts for the Day

TWENTY-FIVE YEARS OF WISDOM

COMPILED BY M.C. Sungaila

Crystal Cove
PRESS

Published by Crystal Cove Press, Newport Beach, California

Edited and designed by Girl Friday Productions
www.girlfridayproductions.com
Design: Paul Barrett

ISBN (hardcover): 978-1-7338657-0-8
ISBN (paperback): 978-1-7338657-1-5

LCCN: 2019939650

PREFACE

From the time I was in college, my mother has sent me bite-size insights, reassurances, and pieces of wisdom on a nearly daily basis.

First, they came in handwritten letters she mailed to my apartment and later my office, neatly printed across stationery she had created expressly for this purpose: "Mother's thought for the day," it said across the top.

When mobile phones took over, she texted me with her "thought" for the day, often including emojis or illustrations she colored in using the Colorfy app.

But no matter what the medium, her words were always just what I needed to hear at just the right time. They might be for you too. A selection of her words of wisdom follows.

Enjoy!

M.C. Sungaila

M.C.

   I found the following saying and wanted to share it with you.

Mother's Thoughts for the Day

Every task is a self-portrait

of the one who
does it.

PEOPLE WHO FEEL GOOD ABOUT THEMSELVES PRODUCE

good
results.

Quality is not accidental;

it results from intelligent effort.

Obstacles

ARE WHAT YOU SEE WHEN YOU TAKE YOUR EYES OFF THE TARGET.

FACTS DO NOT CEASE TO EXIST

BECAUSE THEY ARE IGNORED.

Many who pray "Our Father" on Sunday act like orphans the rest of the week.

(M.C. This little gem has merit, doesn't it? Mother)

There is destiny that makes us brothers: None goes his way alone.

All that we send into the lives of others comes back into our own.

Nice thought, don't you agree?
Love,
Mother

A FRIEND IS SOMEONE WHO WHEN YOU'VE MADE A FOOL OF YOURSELF

DOESN'T THINK YOU DID A PERMANENT JOB.

Take time to dream—hitch your soul to

the stars.

Plan ahead:

IT WASN'T RAINING WHEN NOAH BUILT THE ARK.

Good morale: you keep working even though

your head
says it can't
be done.

TODAY IS THE TOMORROW YOU WORRIED ABOUT

yesterday.

Never let
yesterday

use up too much of today.

Some people improve the world just by being in it.

P.S. I THINK YOU
FALL IN THIS SLOT.

LEAD,
FOLLOW,

OR
GET OUT
OF THE
WAY.

Never do what you cannot ask

God to
bless.

You ought to have a little *fun* in life.

Otherwise every day is like going to the dentist.

NOT EVERYONE AGREES WITH YOU—

THEY COULD BE RIGHT.

ANY TIME THE GOING SEEMS EASY, CHECK AND SEE IF YOU'RE GOING

down hill.

A real friend
is one who
could tell
you many
things—

but doesn't.

YOU MAY THINK YOU'RE AT A

wall—

IT COULD BE A DOOR— THAT'S *all.*

LIFE WILL BRING
MANY ADVENTURES—
GOOD AND BAD—AND
DISAPPOINTMENTS.
YOU ARE *SPECIAL*. TAKE
ALL THAT LIFE HAS TO
OFFER AND MAKE YOUR
TAPESTRY FULL AND
RICH WITH ALL THE
COLORS THAT YOU WILL
GATHER. (SOME WILL
BE DARK COLORS—BUT
THAT WILL MAKE YOUR
TAPESTRY RICHER.)

You are a lovely person and you
don't even know it, and that's part
of what makes you so special.
Love,
Mother

SOMETIMES, YOU HAVE TO GO TO BED WITH

the
enemy.

If you brought
the meat
and potatoes
to the table,

you're the one
who gets to say
how it's
carved up.

YOU DON'T HAVE TO KNOW ALL THE ANSWERS,

BECAUSE YOU WON'T BE ASKED ALL THE QUESTIONS.

NEVER
TRY TO BE
BETTER THAN
SOMEONE
ELSE . . .

BE THE BEST *you* CAN BE.

Make this the best day

ever!

EVERY DAY
IS A NEW
CANVAS—

PAINT IT THE WAY YOU WANT.

New day. New canvas. Fill your canvas. If you do not, it means you didn't do anything that day.

Don't allow others to touch your canvas. It's your canvas. Others can affect how you fill your canvas . . . but they are not allowed to use your brush!

NICE SEEING YOU ARE A GOOD TEAM PLAYER, HONEST, INTEGRITY-TYPE PERSON.

YOU ARE A PERSON OF HIGH VALUES. WE NEED PEOPLE WITH THOSE QUALITIES AROUND.

You can make this work. This is just a challenge.

It's things like this that build your skill sets.

After thinking things through and asking for input,

YOU MUST TRUST YOUR OWN JUDGMENT.

QUOTE FROM ROBERT KENNEDY:

"All of us might wish at times that we lived in a more tranquil world, but we don't.

And if our times
are difficult and
perplexing, so are
they challenging
and filled with
opportunity."

"Coming together
is a beginning;
keeping together
is progress;

working together is success."

WORDS TO DESCRIBE YOU:

relentless, loyal, intelligent, problem solver, resolute, success oriented, thoughtful, accountable, integrity, follows through, leads by example.

IN SHORT,
YOU HAVE CHARACTER.

Character is built. We are not born with it. It is formed by parents, family, church, teachers, good mentors. And by example.

YOU ARE DOING JUST

fine.

BE PROUD OF WHO AND WHAT YOU ARE.

Those who walk with God always reach their destination.

IF YOU HAVE A PULSE, YOU HAVE A *purpose.*

To influence people, or to have even difficult people like you, put a mirror up to them, and reflect back to them how they would like to be seen.

GOD BLESS YOU WITH THE FOOLISHNESS TO THINK THAT YOU CAN MAKE A DIFFERENCE IN THE WORLD,

SO THAT YOU WILL
DO THE THINGS
WHICH OTHERS
TELL YOU CANNOT
BE DONE.

—Franciscan benediction

You have True Grit. I am very proud of you. You keep moving and working through whatever pops up.

You are a great lawyer. You are a great caring person. Let things gel. Ask for God's guidance. You will do the right thing.

YOU ARE GATHERING YOUR BUILDING MATERIALS AND WORKING ON YOUR SKILLS. IT'S ALL GOOD.

KEEP DOING WHAT YOU ARE DOING, WORKING IN YOUR *victory garden.*

You are doing everything you can and, may I add, very well. You are going to do just fine. You are quick, bright and learning all the time.

Not many people I know learn as fast as you do. You have and are continuing to grow.

GOOD JOB, KID.

Don't be scared.

Scared will not allow you to move forward.

What you are doing is super hard. You are doing a good job. You are learning and morphing into a formidable woman.

Remember,
God is with you.

Love you,
Mother

LET EVERYTHING ELSE GO AND focus.

GO OUT THERE AND BREAK A LEG, KID!!!

I hope that when you get married you find that person you would want to be in a foxhole with. Marriage is a long journey, and as with any journey, you will get lost, there will be forks in the road, there will be incredible beautiful places and some bad places. It is good to have a traveling companion you can trust, laugh, cry, and grow with. Your father is right:

CHOOSE WELL.

Keep the faith, kid. God will lead you and take care of you.

Of course, he expects you to work for it.

THERE WILL
BE VERY FEW
THINGS U
CANNOT GET
IF U U WANT IT
BADLY ENOUGH
AND FOCUS.

NOT EVERYONE CAN DO THAT.

You can.

REMEMBER ONE OF COACH WOODEN'S PRINCIPLES OF LIFE:

LIVE EACH DAY AS IF IT WERE YOUR

masterpiece.

Have a great day.

BREAK A LEG!

Take good care of yourself. Get in clean pj's. Have a cup of tea with lemon and honey.

Relax and stay warm!

Get some rest.
Love ♥ my 🌹

They are even prettier today. ❤❤

We cannot lose our faith in doing the

RIGHT THING.

WE ARE
OUT THERE.

Being people
of character IS
important!!

ME:

We are all home. Another long day. Ugh.

MOTHER:

Makes you stronger.

LIFE IS FALLING.

Living is
getting up.

Do your thing, my dear.

Take some deep breathing and just move forward. Love u.

YOU MUST FEEL AS THOUGH AN ELEPHANT HAS BEEN REMOVED FROM YOUR CHEST.

NOW YOU CAN MOVE FORWARD WITH EVEN MORE

confidence.

GOOD JOB. IT'S THINGS LIKE THIS THAT BUILD YOUR SKILL SETS.

I love
you.

I also believe you are a person of high values.

REMEMBER TODAY IS THE

present—

TREAT
IT
LIKE A

Joy to the world!

The Newborn King is born this day.

TIMING IS EVERYTHING,

and then there's LUCK!

You are prepared. You know what you have to do. Do it with confidence and honesty. You are prepared. Now let your mind relax.

Let things flow through your mind freely. Have the **confidence** that you are excellent at what you do. Tomorrow you will be relaxed, alert, confident. A winner.

YOU ARE A WINNER!

Winners do the best, the very best they can do.

That's a winner. You don't leave anything on the table. You do all you can do. That's a winner. A winner looks inside to see if she did everything she could do. That's what makes a winner. I know you do all those things.

YOU ARE A WINNER!!

JUST REMEMBER—
take God's hand
AND WALK IN THERE
WITH CONFIDENCE.
YOU WON'T HAVE A
BETTER PARTNER.

YOU GO, GIRL!

In everyone's life there is a time or two when we question what our place in life is. What does God have in mind for me? I can't tell you. Sometimes we are doing what he wants already. Sometimes we have not reached it yet. We are on a journey. Trust that the Lord will be traveling with us. Trust that he will help us to know what it is we are to do on our journey. I still don't know exactly what I am to do.

You have done good in the things you have done. Who knows how many lives you have affected in what you do? Sometimes we never know. Do the right thing anyway. I wish I could help you figure things out. Maybe you are doing exactly what you were supposed to do until this epiphany. Maybe it means that now that you are aware, you will be able to handle or face more things.

Who knows! Trust in God. Trust in you. Trust that you are doing exactly what you are supposed to be doing and are on your journey.

Don't worry or feel lost. A journey is filled with so many different roads. Some of the roads will be easy. Some hard, some dangerous.

Some roads will take you past beautiful places. Other roads will be dark. Some will meander. Stay on the road.

My dear. "Oh, the places you will go. The things you will see."

Take this journey with gusto, my love. God is there with you. He will help. A few of the roads you have taken were not good ones—that's life. I have seen you get back on better roads. That's ok. So far on your journey, I have seen you grow and become a woman of substance. I am so proud of who you are.

Love you.

SOLDIER ON.

REMEMBER THE LITHUANIAN MOTTO—IF THE HORSE DIES, GET IN FRONT OF THE PLOW AND PULL!

Remember,
The Lord has
a road

for all
of us.

I know you are disappointed. It is not always the best that are called or chosen. You thought that being good alone would do it. Sometimes. Mostly not. You have come very far on your own.

AGAIN, REMEMBER WHAT I'VE TOLD YOU:

check out the street while you are walking—there might be other opportunities you like better.

THE PATH
YOU ARE ON
IS NOT SUCH
A BAD ONE,
MY DEAR.

BE THE BEST THAT YOU CAN BE.

CAN'T DO BETTER THAN THAT!

I love and
respect who
you are and
who you are
evolving into.

You are one of the warriors.

IT'S ALSO ABOUT TIMING, ISN'T IT. SOMETIMES IT'S NOT THERE.

Then I think God intervenes. He says why don't you take a break. Why don't you stop to smell the roses. Take a look at what you thought you wanted. Evaluate. Talk to God. Listen. If you then decide that's what you want above all else, you need to develop a plan. If, after you have done all of the above, you say wow, and wow, I've just become totally aware after all these years of wanting to do something and I realize that now, not so much—move onward with your life adventure. The best is yet to come!

MARK TWAIN:

"I never allowed my schooling to get in the way of my education."

SOUND ADVICE.

I just wanted you to know I am so in awe of you so much of the time!

You just pick
yourself up and
push forward. You
are made of the
right stuff,
my dear

THOUGHT
FOR THE DAY:

"Never grow a wishbone where a backbone ought to be."

Stay centered.

Stay balanced.

M.C.,

A NEW YEAR IS HERE. MAKE IT THE BEST ONE EVER!

Each year will be filled with good—not so good—and just awful. That's life. It's how you deal with these things that define you. Not the things.

When you were younger I was concerned because you are so sensitive. I am no longer concerned. I have seen you go down hard. After you clear your head, you think about what has happened, what went wrong, and what you will do.

You pick yourself up and move forward. No, I am not concerned. You have learned the lesson of that quote I sent you . . . life is falling down; living is getting up and moving forward.

NO, I AM NOT CONCERNED. I KNOW YOU HAVE
the right stuff.

Make this the best year ever. Fill this year with love, fun, and lots of adventures. Oh, and don't forget challenges. CHALLENGES HELP YOU GROW.

MOTHER

ABOUT THE AUTHOR

M.C. Sungaila lives and works in Orange County, California, where she grew up. Her mother does too.

9 781733 865708